THE LEARNING REVOLUTION

THE LEARNING REVOLUTION

Transforming Education for the Digital Age

B. VINCENT

QuantumQuill Press

CONTENTS

Introduction: The Dawn of the Digital Education Era

Historical Context and Evolution of Educational Practices

Education, the cornerstone of civilization's progress, has passed through a gorgeous evolution from the oral traditions of historical societies to the massive digital lecture rooms of the 21st century. This ride mirrors humanity's relentless pursuit of understanding and its transmission throughout generations. In historic times, schooling used to be a distinctive privilege, constrained inside the partitions of sacred temples and the courts of the elite. The expertise imparted used to be esoteric, reserved for a select few deemed valuable of its secrets. These early academic practices had been deeply intertwined with the social, political, and non-secular fabric of the time, reflecting the hierarchical shape of society.

As civilizations advanced, so did their academic systems. The invention of writing used to be a pivotal milestone, remodeling the transmission of knowledge. It allowed for the maintenance of thoughts, discoveries, and teachings, enabling them to attain a wider target audience beyond the constraints of time and space. This democratization of know-how laid the groundwork for the scholarly traditions of historic Greece, and the library of Alexandria, the place of study and inquiry, has been celebrated.

The Middle Ages added about the institution of universities, establishments devoted to the pursuit of know-how in a number of disciplines. These facilities for gaining knowledge grew to become beacons of mental activity, nurturing the minds that would propel humanity into the Renaissance. For the duration of this period, education started to shake off the shackles of exclusivity, although it remained mainly for the affluent.

The Industrial Revolution ushered in a new technology of academic reform, pushed by the needs of an evolving workforce. Public training structures had been established, recognizing the necessity of a skilled populace for societal advancement. The study room grew to become a microcosm of democratic ideals, a location where understanding was once not simply a privilege but a right.

In the twentieth century, technological developments commenced to reshape training as soon as again. Radio, television, and, eventually, the internet multiplied the horizons of learning, making it viable to attain rookies in each nook of the globe. The digital age has modified the panorama of education, breaking down the partitions of the lecture room and introducing a new technology where expertise is accessible, interactive, and limitless.

This historic trip from the temples of historical civilizations to the digital school rooms of these days underscores a crucial truth: training is a living, respiratory entity, evolving with society. The dawn of the digital schooling generation is now not basically a chapter in this ongoing saga, but a substantial soar forward, promising to redefine its capacity to learn, teach, and share expertise in the contemporary world.

Technological Milestones and Their Impact on Learning

The march of growth in schooling has been inexorably linked to the developments in technology; every bounce ahead in our capacity to manipulate the world around us is mirrored with the aid of a sore ahead in how we impart and take in knowledge. The printing press, invented with the aid of Johannes Gutenberg in the fifteenth century, stands as one of the most transformative technological milestones in the realm of education. This invention revolutionized the dissemination of knowledge, making books more accessible and affordable, thereby democratizing learning. It used to be a radical departure from the painstakingly gradual procedure of hand-copying texts, which now not solely restrained the manufacturing and distribution of understanding but additionally saved it ensconced inside the elite and the clergy. The printing press broke down these barriers, heralding a technology where expertise ought to unfold and flourish more freely.

As we transitioned into the twentieth century, the introduction of digital media accelerated the tempo of academic transformation. The radio, delivered to the public in the early 1900s, grew to become a novel instructional device by using the Nineteen Twenties and 1930s to bring lectures, instructional programs, and new thoughts into residences and lecture rooms throughout the globe. It was once a precursor to the instructional television of the mid-20th century, which sought to mix visible knowledge with accessibility, attaining college students in far-off places and offering a complement to ordinary schoolroom instruction.

The genuine paradigm shift, however, arrived with the creation of the laptop and the internet. The private computer, which became extensive in the 1980s, and the World Wide Web, which exploded in the 1990s, collectively initiated a technology of exceptional access to information. These applied sciences dismantled geographical and temporal obstacles to education, enabling every person with a web connection to get entry to enormous repositories of knowledge, examine new skills, and even attend virtual classrooms.

Online studying systems and Massive Open Online Courses (MOOCs) emerged as beacons of this new digital training frontier, supplying publications from prestigious universities to inexperienced persons worldwide at little or no cost. This democratization of greater training represented a seismic shift in how expertise used to be accessed and consumed, making lifelong study a workable truth for millions.

The influence of these technological milestones on studying has been profound and multifaceted. They have now not solely improved admission to training but additionally enriched the mastering trip by making it more interactive, engaging, and tailor-made to character needs. Technology has converted the teacher's function from the sole source of understanding to a facilitator of learning, guiding college students via a sizeable digital panorama stuffed with data and possibilities for discovery.

As we stand on the cusp of new advances in synthetic intelligence, digital and augmented reality, and different rising technologies, it is clear that the journey of instructional transformation is a long way from over. Each new technological milestone brings with it the potential to revolutionize education, making it more immersive, personalized, and reachable than ever before. The story of science and training is one of mutual advancement, a narrative of how human ingenuity in harnessing the equipment of our advent has continuously reshaped the approaches in which we analyze and teach.

Identifying the Catalysts for a Learning Revolution

In the ever-evolving narrative of education, the transition toward digital technology does not now show up in isolation. It used to be propelled through a confluence of catalysts, each signaling an urgent desire for a transformation in how we studied and taught. These catalysts, rising from the shortcomings of usual instructional models, technological advancements, and moving societal needs, have jointly ushered in the dawn of the knowledge revolution.

The Limitations of Traditional Education Systems: At the coronary heart of the push toward digital schooling is the developing cognizance of the obstacles inherent in typical instructional systems. These systems, mostly unchanged for decades, have regularly been criticized for their one-size-fits-all approach, which fails to accommodate the various needs and gain knowledge of the styles and paces of individual students. The industrial mannequin of education, characterized by standardized trying out and uniform curricula, has increasingly been considered insufficient for getting college students ready for the complexities of the modern-day world. This mismatch between what is taught in regular lecture rooms and the capabilities required in the twenty-first century has highlighted the need for a more flexible, adaptable, and customized approach to education.

The Role of Technology in Highlighting Educational Gaps: The speedy development of science has no longer solely furnished the equipment for a digital schooling transformation but has additionally performed a pivotal role in highlighting the gaps in common instructional models. Digital equipment and sources have made it feasible to get right of entry to a wealth of records and getting to know possibilities beyond the classroom, showcasing the viable for a greater dynamic, interactive, and personalized getting to know experience. As technological know-how continues to permeate every aspect of society, the distinction between the static nature of normal schooling and the dynamic skills of digital mastery has become increasingly stark, underscoring the urgency for academic reform.

Emerging Needs of Students and Educators: The catalysts for the study revolution additionally stem from the evolving wishes of college students and educators themselves. Today's novices are digital natives, accustomed to the immediacy and interactivity of the digital world. Their expectations for engagement, collaboration, and immediacy in comments are reshaping the instructional landscape, requiring stressful educational methodologies that are extra aligned with these digital experiences. Similarly, educators are in search of greater wonderful potential to interact with students, check their growth in real-time, and tailor practice to meet man or woman needs, all of which are facilitated via digital technologies.

A Globalized World Demanding New Skills: The shift in the direction of a knowledge-based, globalized economic system has similarly underscored the necessity for a study revolution. In this context, the capability to think critically, collaborate across cultures, and adapt to fast change is as vital as typical educational knowledge. Digital education, with its emphasis on imperative thinking, problem-solving, and digital literacy, affords a pathway to obtaining these 21st-century skills, making it an imperative issue of academic reform.

The Quest for Equity and Access: Finally, the push in the direction of digital schooling is pushed by means of a quest for increased fairness and access to education. Traditional instructional structures frequently replicate societal inequalities, with the right of entry to excellent training carefully tied to socioeconomic status. Digital education, on the other hand, holds the promise of leveling the playing field and imparting splendid mastering possibilities to college students regardless of their geographical region or monetary background.

These catalysts, woven together, have created a compelling case for a getting-to-know revolution. They signify a collective consciousness that the future of schooling lies now not inside the confines of typical school rooms but in the boundless, dynamic chances of the digital age. As we navigate this transition, it is these catalysts that inform our journey, making it difficult for us to reimagine training for a new era.

The Promises of Digital Age Education

The dawn of digital schooling technology brings with it guarantees that have the manageability to redefine the panorama of learning. These promises, grounded in technology's potential to transcend usual barriers, provide an imaginative and prescient form of schooling that is more accessible, engaging, and tailor-made to the wishes of each and every learner. As we delve into the transformative abilities of digital education, it will become clear that these guarantees are now not mere aspirations but rather tangible chances ready to be realized.

Enhanced Accessibility to Quality Education: One of the most compelling guarantees of digital schooling is the democratization of access to first-rate study resources. With the introduction of online platforms, instructional materials that were once limited to prestigious establishments or geographically far-off areas are now reachable to all and sundry with a net connection. This unparalleled stage of accessibility opens doorways for inexperienced people around the globe, breaking down the socioeconomic obstacles that have historically hindered instructional equity. The promise of established right of entry to training is a cornerstone of the digital getting to know revolution, providing hope for a more knowledgeable and trained international society.

Engagement and Interactivity: Digital training transforms the passive getting-to-know-mannequin of standard school rooms into an interactive, attractive experience. Through multimedia content, digital simulations, and interactive modules, beginners can discover topics in depth, making use of ideas in digital environments that mimic real-world scenarios. This hands-on strategy now not only makes mastering more fascinating but additionally enhances retention and understanding. The promise of an extra-engaged approach to gaining knowledge of systems speaks to the coronary heart of education's purpose: to ignite an ardor for discovery and foster a deep, lasting grasp of the world.

Personalization and Adaptability: Perhaps the most transformative promise of digital schooling lies in its potential to tailor studying experiences to the character wants of every student. Adaptive mastering applied sciences analyzes learners' responses in real-time, adjusting the situational degree and imparting new challenges at the proper pace. This personalized strategy ensures that college students continue to be neither bored by using cloth that's too effortless nor overwhelmed by content material that is too difficult. It acknowledges the special ride of every learner, promising an extra-inclusive and fine instructional experience.

Preparation for the Digital World: As we navigate the complexities of the twenty-first century, the capabilities required for success extend beyond normal tutorial knowledge. Digital literacy, quintessential thinking, and the capacity to collaborate throughout digital structures are becoming more vital. The digital schooling generation guarantees to equip newcomers with these crucial skills, making them ready for the challenges and possibilities of a digital world. This alignment of instructional effects with the needs of cutting-edge society ensures that rookies are now not simply shoppers of expertise but energetic members of the digital landscape.

Innovative Pedagogies and Collaborative Learning: Finally, digital training opens the door to modern educational methodologies that foster collaboration and creativity. Online forums, collaborative projects, and peer evaluation structures leverage the collective genius of the learner community, encouraging college students to examine one another. This collaborative method mirrors the interconnectedness of the digital age, promising an education that is now not solely about obtaining information but also about constructing relationships and grasping numerous perspectives.

The guarantees of digital age schooling replicate an imaginative and prescient way of studying that is inclusive, engaging, and aligned with the desires of a hastily altering world. As we include the probabilities of this new era, these guarantees inform our efforts, imparting a blueprint for a schooling device that prepares all newcomers to thrive in the digital age.

Challenges and Resistance Facing the Shift to Digital Education

While the dawn of digital education technology is replete with promises, it additionally confronts a panorama of challenges and resistance that need to be navigated with care and strategic foresight. These challenges, rising from logistical constraints and deeply ingrained perceptions of education, pose huge hurdles to the full cognizance of digital learning's potential. Understanding these challenges is crucial, not as a deterrent but as a roadmap for overcoming the boundaries that stand in the way of reworking schooling for the digital age.

Bridging the Digital Divide: At the forefront of these challenges is the digital divide, a chronic hole between those who get admission to digital applied sciences and the web and those who do not. This divide extends beyond mere bodily right of entry to consist of disparities in digital literacy and the capacity to efficaciously use technological know-how for learning. Addressing this divide is critical to making sure that the shift to digital training does not exacerbate current inequalities but rather serves as a bridge to higher academic equity.

Ensuring Accessibility for Diverse Learners: Digital training ought to be inclusive, catering to the wants of all learners, along with those with disabilities. This requires a sketch of handy substances and systems that comply with normal plan principles, making sure that digital schooling is a device for empowerment and no longer exclusion. The assignment lies in embedding accessibility into the fabric of digital education, making it a foundational alternative rather than an afterthought.

Balancing Technological Integration with Pedagogical Effectiveness: The attraction of new applied sciences can now and again overshadow the pedagogical ideas that must inform their use in education. There is a subtle stability to be struck between leveraging technological know-how to get to know and making sure that technological equipment serves pedagogical goals; no longer exchange them. Educators face the assignment of integrating technological know-how in a way that enriches the gaining knowledge of the journey, besides diluting the essence of instructing and the human connection that is integral to a good education.

Safeguarding Privacy and Data Security: With the growing use of digital structures for learning, worries about privacy and statistics safety have come to the fore. The series and evaluation of learner data, while priceless for personalizing education, additionally increases big privacy concerns. The venture is to advance strong fact-protection measures and obvious insurance policies that shield learner information, constructing faith in digital training systems.

Overcoming Resistance to Change: Finally, the shift to digital schooling encounters resistance rooted in standard views of education and learning. For educators, parents, and even some students, the transition from traditional lecture room settings to online systems represents a profound exchange in the instructional experience. Overcoming this resistance requires demonstrating the cost of digital education, imparting assistance and coaching for educators, and fostering a lifestyle of innovation inside academic institutions.

These challenges, as daunting as they may additionally seem, are no longer insurmountable. They characterize the developing pains of a transformative shift in how training is delivered and experienced. By addressing these challenges head-on, with a dedication to equity, inclusivity, and pedagogical effectiveness, the transition to digital training can fulfill its promise to revolutionize mastering for the digital age. This trip requires collaboration, innovation, and a steadfast trust in the energy of schooling to transcend obstacles and release the potential of each learner.

Chapter 1: Foundations of Digital Learning

Theoretical Frameworks Supporting Digital Education

At the coronary heart of digital training lies a prosperous tapestry of theoretical frameworks that inform its design, implementation, and evaluation. These frameworks are no longer mere educational constructs; they serve as the bedrock upon which nice and transformative digital learning environments are built. Understanding these theories is imperative for educators, designers, and policymakers alike as they navigate the complexities of integrating technological know-how into instructional practices.

Constructivism stands as a pillar in the theoretical basis of digital education. This principle posits that newcomers assemble know-how via their experiences as a substitute for passively receiving information. Digital environments, with their interactive and immersive capabilities, grant a fertile floor for constructivist learning, permitting college students to explore, experiment, and discover. The interactive simulations, digital labs, and collaborative tasks facilitated via digital equipment exemplify the constructivist method in action, enabling rookies to construct appreciation in a context that mirrors real-world scenarios.

Connectivism, a concept for the digital age, emphasizes the role of networks and connections in learning. It suggests that understanding is dispensed throughout a community of connections, and studying happens through navigating and engaging with these networks. Digital education, with its online forums, social media, and collaborative platforms, embodies the ideas of connectivism, enabling novices to join with information, resources, and communities beyond the common classroom. This idea highlights the significance of digital literacy and the capability to curate, create, and share know-how inside digital ecosystems.

The socio-cultural approach to gaining knowledge similarly enriches our grasp of digital education. This point of view focuses on the social contexts of mastering and the function of interaction, culture, and neighborhood in shaping academic experiences. Digital structures facilitate social gaining of knowledge via enabling discussions, peer feedback, and collaboration amongst newcomers from numerous backgrounds. This method emphasizes the importance of cultural variety and social interplay in learning, promoting a more inclusive and globally related instructional experience.

These theoretical frameworks, at the same time, underscore a shift from teacher-centered to learner-centered paradigms in education. Digitally gaining knowledge of environments, by using their very nature, aids in a learner-centered approach, imparting customized pathways, bendy pacing, and possibilities for lively engagement. They motivate freshmen to take possession of their studying journey, fostering a sense of autonomy and a lifelong mastering mindset.

As we delve deeper into the foundations of digital learning, it becomes evident that these theoretical frameworks are no longer simply summary thoughts but rather sensible publications that inform each element of digital education. From the sketch of online guides to the resolution of instructional applied sciences and the advent of mastering communities, these theories supply a roadmap for developing meaningful, effective, and transformative mastering experiences in the digital age.

Key Technologies Driving Educational Innovation

The panorama of digital getting to know is always reshaped and enriched through a suite of key technologies, each taking part in a pivotal position in the evolution of academic practices. These applied sciences no longer solely facilitate the shipping of content material but additionally seriously change the very nature of learning, making it extra interactive, accessible, and personalized. As we discover these technological drivers, we find the profound influence they have on instructional innovation, presenting a glimpse into the future of learning.

Learning management systems (LMS) serve as the spine of digital education, imparting a structured environment in which educators can create, deliver, and manipulate instructional content. LMS systems like Canvas, Moodle, and Blackboard exemplify how technological know-how can streamline the instructional process, imparting facets such as direction management, grading systems, and dialogue forums. These systems embody the shift toward extra-geared-up and available digital mastering experiences, enabling educators and college students to navigate the complexities of online schooling with ease.

Cloud computing has emerged as a transformative force in digital education, democratizing access to computing sources and storage. Cloud-based offerings allow novices and educators to get access to direction materials, put up assignments, and collaborate in real-time, regardless of geographical constraints. This technological know-how helps create a seamless studying experience where academic assets are constantly available, up-to-date, and secure, fostering a flexible mastering environment that adapts to the wants of every learner.

Mobile technologies have revolutionized the way we get access to information, and their effect on training is no less significant. Smartphones and pills provide the ultimate in comfort and portability, permitting freshmen to get access to academic content material anytime, anywhere. Mobile getting-to-know apps and systems cater to a large variety of getting-to-know patterns and preferences, incorporating multimedia content, interactive quizzes, and gamification factors to interact with newbies in a dynamic and personalized getting-to-know journey.

The horizons of instructional science are similarly improved with the aid of emerging technologies such as artificial intelligence (AI), virtual reality (VR), and augmented reality (AR). AI-powered systems can supply personalized mastering experiences via adaptive gaining knowledge of paths that respond to the person's tempo and performance. VR and AR, on the other hand, provide immersive learning experiences that bring complicated topics to life, offering beginners digital environments in which they can explore, experiment, and engage in methods that were previously unimaginable.

The practical effects of these applied sciences on education are profound. They provide possibilities for engagement, personalization, and accessibility in difficult academic fashions, opening up new avenues for learning. However, the integration of these applied sciences additionally poses challenges, requiring considerate consideration of pedagogical objectives, technological infrastructure, and equitable access to make sure that the promise of instructional innovation is realized for all learners.

As we proceed to navigate the evolving panorama of digital learning, it is clear that these key applied sciences are now not only equipment but catalysts for change, using instructional innovation and shaping the future of learning in the digital age.

Principles of Effective Digital Learning Design

In the giant expanse of digital education, the graph of mastering experiences stands as a crucial determinant of their effectiveness. Crafting these experiences requires more than simply an appreciation of the situation; it requires a deep understanding of how humans research in digital environments and the ideas that inform the advent of engaging, meaningful, and on-hand study opportunities. These principles, rooted in each pedagogy and technology, provide a blueprint for educators and designers striving to maximize the plausibility of digital learning.

Interactivity is the lifeblood of superb digital knowledge of design. Interactive factors such as quizzes, simulations, and dialogue boards radically change passive content consumption into lively getting-to-know experiences. By engaging immediately with the material, inexperienced people assemble their understanding more deeply, exploring ideas via action and reflection. Interactivity additionally extends to the social dimension of learning, where peer interactions enrich the mastering process, supplying various views and fostering a sense of community.

Flexibility in studying layout addresses the various needs, backgrounds, and patterns of students. Digital education, with its potential for customization, lets in newbies navigate content material at their own pace, revisit difficult concepts, and get entry to assist assets as needed. This precept ensures that mastery is now not a one-size-fits-all trip but rather a personalized trip that adapts to the character learner's tempo and preferences.

User-Centered Design emphasizes the significance of designing digitally to gain knowledge of experiences with the learner's needs, abilities, and context in mind. This strategy entails intuitive navigation, clear instructions, and on-hand content, making sure that the digital studying environment is inclusive and supportive of all learners. A user-centered sketch additionally entails ongoing comments from rookies to refine and enhance the studying experience, making it more responsive to their evolving needs.

Engagement is a cornerstone of advantageous digital learning, taking pictures of the learner's activity and sustaining their motivation during the learning journey. Engaging digital content material frequently accommodates multimedia elements, storytelling, and real-world functions that make getting to know it applicable and meaningful. By connecting instructional content material to the learner's hobbies and experiences, digital learning can ignite curiosity and encourage an ardor for lifelong learning.

Pedagogically, sound diagrams are possibly the most foundational principle, making sure that the use of technological know-how enhances rather than detracts from the mastering experience. This precept entails aligning digital content material and things to do with getting to know objectives, using evidence-based educational strategies, and integrating evaluation in a way that helps learning. A pedagogically sound graph ensures that technological know-how serves the dreams of education, fostering deep perception and indispensable questioning skills.

These standards of positive digital learning format are no longer standalone concerns but interwoven threads that create a wealthy tapestry of instructional experiences. By adhering to these guidelines, educators and designers can create digital getting-to-know environments that are no longer solely technologically superior but additionally deeply human, advertising getting-to-know that is engaging, accessible, and transformative. As we proceed to discover the chances of digital education, these concepts inform our efforts, making sure that the digital studying revolution fulfills its promise to decorate schooling for freshmen everywhere.

Blended Learning Models

In the evolving narrative of digital education, blended study fashions emerge as a harmonious synthesis of common and digital educational methodologies. These models, characterized by the considerate integration of face-to-face guidance with online learning, signify a pragmatic approach to the complexities of contemporary education. They recognized the enduring cost of direct teacher-student interactions while harnessing the energy of technological know-how to increase and enrich the studying experience. This chapter delves into the essence of blended learning, exploring more than a few fashions and the special advantages they provide to the academic landscape.

The Flipped Classroom Mannequin stands out for its modern inversion of typical school room dynamics. In this approach, inexperienced persons have interaction with academic content material online and in the classroom, freeing up in-class time for interactive activities, discussions, and personalized support. This mannequin shifts the focal point from passive listening to lively learning, permitting instructors to commit greater time to addressing students' wishes and fostering a deeper appreciation of the material. The flipped lecture room no longer solely enhances learner engagement but additionally encourages autonomy as college students take extra duty for their mastering journey.

Hybrid learning, like every other key mannequin of blended education, combines online and in-person studying in a way that enhances the other. Unlike the flipped classroom, hybrid learning does not prescribe a unique sequence for online and face-to-face interactions; however, as an alternative, it presents flexibility in how these factors are integrated. This mannequin caters to the various wishes of learners, accommodating specific getting-to-know patterns and schedules. It additionally presents possibilities for scalability, accomplishing newbies who might also now not be in a position to attend ordinary lessons due to geographical or logistical constraints.

Integrated digital models symbolize the frontier of blended learning, the place where digital science is seamlessly woven into each component of the academic process. These fashions leverage the modern day in instructional technology, from AI-driven personalized getting-to-know paths to collaborative online platforms, to create a mastering environment that is both dynamic and inclusive. Integrated digital fashions are characterized by their adaptability, presenting personalized studying experiences that alter in real-time to the learner's growth and needs.

The exploration of these blended study fashions exhibits a frequent theme: the pursuit of balance. Balancing the richness of face-to-face interactions with the flexibility and accessibility of online learning creates an extra-holistic instructional experience. This stability is now not static but dynamic, evolving with advances in science and shifts in academic philosophy.

Benefits and challenges related to blended mastering tactics underscore the complexity of enforcing these models. Benefits consist of multiplied engagement, accessibility, and personalization, as well as the manageable for extra environment-friendly use of instructional resources. However, challenges such as the want for strong technological infrastructure, expert improvement for educators, and techniques to make sure fairness in getting right of entry to science have to be addressed to realize the full attainable of blended learning.

Case studies showcasing the profitable implementation of blended learning in numerous instructional settings provide treasured insights into sensible application. These real-world examples illustrate how blended mastering fashions can be tailored to specific contexts, highlighting the techniques that have led to high-quality integration of digital and ordinary instructing methods.

As we navigate the future of education, blended learning and gaining knowledge of fashion stand as beacons of innovation, presenting a pathway to a greater engaging, flexible, and inclusive mastering experience. The exploration of these fashions no longer solely enriches our appreciation of the chances of digital schooling, but additionally challenges us to reimagine the shape and meaning of studying in the digital age.

Case Studies of Successful Digital Learning Implementation

In the panorama of digital education, ideas and exercises converge in the form of case research that illuminates the direction to profitable implementation. These real-world examples serve as beacons, guiding educators, policymakers, and innovators through the intricacies of digital learning. By analyzing the successes and challenges encountered by a range of academic institutions around the globe, we glean useful insights into the sensible software of digitally gaining knowledge of principles. This exploration no longer solely highlights the transformative viability of digital training but additionally sheds light on the techniques that can facilitate its nice integration into numerous getting-to-know environments.

Rural School District Transformation: One compelling case to learn about emerges from a rural college district that leveraged digital knowledge to overcome geographic isolation and restrained resources. By equipping each pupil with a pill and making sure dependable net get admission to via neighborhood partnerships, the district created a blended learning environment that linked college students with world resources. The initiative led to giant enhancements in pupil engagement and achievement, illustrating how science can democratize the right of entry to fine education.

University-Level Online Learning Initiative: Another instance entails a principal college that launched a complete online learning application aimed at extending its reach to non-traditional students. Through an aggregate of synchronous and asynchronous courses, the college supplied flexible getting-to-know preferences for working adults, navy personnel, and worldwide students. This case demonstrates the scalability of digital studying and its ability to smash down obstacles to greater education.

Vocational Training by way of Virtual Reality: A groundbreaking strategy to vocational coaching concerned the use of digital fact (VR) simulations to instruct complicated technical skills. This initiative supplied newcomers with an immersive, hands-on trip in a protected and managed environment, improving talent acquisition and retention. The success of this software underscores the practicality of rising applied sciences to revolutionize vocational training.

Global Collaborative Learning Project: Highlighting the connective electricity of digital education, a world collaborative gaining knowledge of assignments introduced collectively college students from exceptional nations to work on joint projects. Utilizing digital systems for conversation and collaboration, college students developed cross-cultural grasp and teamwork skills. This case exemplifies the practicability of digitally gaining knowledge to foster international citizenship and collaboration.

Personalized Learning in a Public School System: Finally, a public faculty system's implementation of a personalized mastering platform showcases the capacity of digital tools to cater to man or woman's needs. By using records analytics to tailor education and supply real-time feedback, the device makes it more advantageous for scholars to gain knowledge of consequences and instructor effectiveness. This instance illustrates the transformative effect of adaptively studying applied sciences on normal academic models.

Each of these case studies presents a special viewpoint on the profitable implementation of digital learning, highlighting numerous techniques that tackle unique challenges and objectives. From leveraging science to bridge geographic divides to making use of modern equipment for talent development, these examples provide a roadmap for educators and establishments in search of ways to navigate the digital training landscape. Moreover, they underscore the significance of adaptability, collaboration, and a dedication to fairness in realizing the full potential of digital learning. As we move forward, these case studies no longer solely serve as concepts but additionally as sensible courses in the ongoing experience to seriously change training for the digital age.

Chapter 2: Personalized Learning in the Digital Age

Understanding personalized learning

In the digital age, the idea of personalized learning stands as a beacon of innovation in the academic landscape, promising a departure from the traditional, one-size-fits-all method to an extra-individualized academic experience. At its core, customized learning is an instructional approach aimed at tailoring coaching to the special needs, skills, and pastimes of every learner. This method now not solely acknowledges but also celebrates the range amongst learners, recognizing that every student's journey to expertise is as special as their fingerprint.

The Shift from Traditional Models: For centuries, schooling structures have operated on a standardized model, where curriculum, pacing, and evaluation have been uniforming for all students. This model, which is environment-friendly for its time, regularly disregarded the character variations in studying styles, speed, and hobbies of students. Personalized learning, on the other hand, seeks to dismantle these one-size-fits-all structures, changing them and gaining knowledge of paths that adapt to the learner, no longer the other way around.

The Role of Learner Profiles: Central to the personalized mastering method is the introduction of certain learner profiles. These profiles are dynamic, data-rich snapshots of every student's strengths, weaknesses, preferences, and goals. They serve as the basis for personalizing academic experience, guiding educators in tailoring instruction and resources, and helping to meet the special desires of every student. Through non-stop updates and reflections, these pro-files evolve, gaining knowledge of the journey's nuances and making sure that the instructional trip stays aligned with the learner's boom and altering needs.

The Importance of the Digital Age: The creation of digital applied sciences has propelled customized getting to know from concept to practice, supplying the equipment and assets crucial to putting in force individualized getting to know at scale. In an age marked by speedy technological development and an increasing number of numerous instructional needs, customized mastery gives a pathway to extra equitable, effective, and enticing education. It acknowledges the learner now not as a passive recipient of information but as an energetic participant in their academic journey, empowered to explore, discover, and form their knowledge of experience.

Personalized studying in the digital age is no longer, in simple terms, an instructional method but rather a profound reimagining of the studying process. It challenges regular paradigms, embraces the possibility of technology, and places the learner at the heart of education. By grasping the foundational standards of personalized learning, educators, policymakers, and technologists can commence to free up its transformative potential, paving the way for a future where training is no longer simply a shared trip but a private voyage of discovery for each learner.

Technology's Role in Tailoring Education to Individual Needs

The transformative electricity of personalized learning in the digital age is inextricably linked to the developments in technological know-how that have made such individualized schooling now not solely achievable but eminently achievable. As we delve into the function of science in tailoring training to man or woman's needs, we find a panorama of the place innovation meets instruction, developing a synergy that propels the personalization of gaining knowledge.

Digital Tools and Platforms: The proliferation of digital equipment and systems has been an indispensable enabler of personalized learning. Learning management systems (LMS), adaptive studying software, and academic apps provide an array of functionalities designed to aid custom-made getting-to-know experiences. These structures can dynamically alter content, pace, and complexity based totally on real-time remarks from the learner, making sure that every scholar is engaged with a fabric that is both difficult and achievable. Furthermore, digital portfolios permit college students and educators to track their development over time, presenting a holistic view of their achievements and areas for improvement.

Adaptive Learning Technologies: At the forefront of technological developments in training are adaptive learning technologies. These state-of-the-art structures make use of algorithms to analyze a learner's interactions and performance, adjusting the mastering pathway in response to the learner's needs. By constantly assessing a student's perception and talent level, adaptive applied sciences can provide just-in-time resources, remediation, and challenges, making sure that studying is optimized for every individual's tempo and capabilities.

Impact of Data Analytics and AI: The integration of data analytics and artificial intelligence (AI) in instructional equipment represents a quantum leap in the ability for personalization. Through the series and evaluation of giant quantities of gaining knowledge of data, AI can become aware of patterns and insights that inform personalized mastering strategies. For instance, AI can advise assets that align with a student's gaining knowledge of fashion or predict areas where a scholar can also face challenges, permitting preemptive intervention. This data-driven method no longer solely enhances the precision of personalization but additionally opens new avenues for appreciation of how college students examine best.

The position of technological know-how in personalizing training extends beyond the mere provision of custom-made content. It encompasses a broader imaginative and prescient view of academic surroundings that respects and responds to the individuality of every learner. Through digital tools, adaptive technologies, and AI, educators are outfitted to meet the various desires of their students, fostering a study tradition that values growth, engagement, and the pursuit of private excellence.

As we discover the confluence of science and personalized learning, it becomes evident that the digital age presents unheard-of possibilities to radically change education. By harnessing the attainable capabilities of these technologies, educators can create getting-to-know experiences that now not solely adapt to the wishes of male or female college students but additionally empower them to take charge of their academic journey, making studying more relevant, engaging, and effective.

Data-Driven Approaches to Personalization

In the realm of customized learning, records stand as the linchpin, enabling an academic strategy that is as dynamic and multifaceted as the novices it seeks to serve. The creation of data-driven methodologies in training heralds a new generation where decisions, interventions, and educational techniques are knowledgeable by using deep insights into the process of gaining knowledge. This method harnesses the energy of information to tailor training to the desires of students, marking a significant departure from traditional, intuition-based instructional practices.

The Significance of Data Collection and Analysis: At the coronary heart of data-driven personalization is the systematic series and evaluation of facts associated with scholar performance, engagement, and study preferences. This data, gathered through digital platforms, assessments, and learner interactions, gives a wealth of insights that educators can use to apprehend and assist every student's getting-to-know journey. By inspecting patterns and developments inside this data, educators can discover areas of power and challenge, tailor educational content, and furnish focused guidance for the places they are most wanted.

Ethical Considerations and Best Practices in Handling Student Data: As we navigate the conceivable amount of information to radically change education, we also need to tread cautiously with the moral issues it entails. Privacy, consent, and protection are paramount, necessitating a framework of great practices that protect students' data while leveraging it for their benefit. Educators and technologists have to collaborate to make certain that records series and evaluation are performed with transparency, respecting the privacy rights of inexperienced persons, and keeping the easiest requirements of information security.

Examples of Effective Data-Driven Strategies: The utility of data-driven techniques in customized learning manifests in a number of modern practices. Adaptive getting-to-know platforms, for example, make use of real-time records to modify the problem of tasks, making sure that college students are constantly challenged, barring being overwhelmed. Predictive analytics can forecast viable getting-to-know obstacles, permitting preemptive intervention. Moreover, information visualization equipment can supply college students and educators with on-the-spot remarks on progress, facilitating an extra responsive and knowledgeable studying experience.

The promise of data-driven strategies for personalization is now not in basic terms in the customization of schooling to man or woman learner profiles, but in the ability to unearth deeper insights into how gaining knowledge occurs. By embedding statistical evaluation into the material of instructional practices, we can discover the nuances of getting to know styles, the efficacy of academic strategies, and the influence of a number of interventions. This knowledge, in turn, empowers educators to craft studying experiences that are no longer solely customized but additionally deeply resonant with the wishes and aspirations of their students.

As we forge ahead in the digital age, the integration of data-driven methodologies in personalized knowledge acquisition stands as a testimony to the conceivable use of technological know-how to beautify human perception and capability. It underscores a dedication to a schooling gadget that values and responds to the individuality of every learner, paving the way for a future where each scholar has the probability of attaining their fullest potential.

Challenges and Solutions in Personalized Learning

The experience closer to totally realizing customized learning in the digital age is fraught with challenges, every one of which presents barriers to the seamless integration of individualized education. Yet, with each project comes a suite of solutions, born from innovation, dedication, and a deep dedication to instructional equity. This exploration into the hurdles of personalized mastering and the techniques to overcome them illuminates the course forward, imparting hope and a route for educators, technologists, and policymakers alike.

Technological Barriers: One of the primary challenges in the implementation of personalized learning is the technological barrier. Not all establishments have the infrastructure, resources, or access to the digital equipment critical to personalized knowledge of environments. To bridge this digital divide, strategic investments in instructional science are essential, coupled with partnerships between instructional institutions, science companies, and government agencies. Training packages for educators to effectively make use of digital equipment can additionally play a pivotal role in overcoming technological barriers.

Pedagogical Adjustments: The shift to customized studying requires an essential rethinking of instructional methodologies. Traditional pedagogical processes are regularly ill-suited to the dynamic, learner-centered paradigms of customized education. Educators should consequently include new academic techniques that prioritize flexibility, scholar agency, and the integration of science into the mastering process. Professional improvement programs, peer-gaining knowledge of communities, and getting right of entry to a repository of pleasant practices can guide instructors in this transition, making sure they are well-equipped to navigate the complexities of customized learning.

Logistical Considerations: Implementing personalized knowledge at scale includes logistical challenges, from type scheduling to the allocation of resources. Solutions consist of leveraging science to streamline administrative processes, adopting flexible scheduling structures that accommodate character-gaining knowledge of paths, and designing bodily mastering areas that assist assorted mastering activities. Collaborative planning amongst educators, administrators, and college students can additionally make sure that logistical preparations are aligned with the desires of personalized learning.

Facilitating Educator Roles: As customized mastering emphasizes the learner's autonomy, the function of the educator evolves from that of an information dispenser to that of a guide, mentor, and facilitator. This transformation necessitates a reevaluation of trainer coaching and expert development, emphasizing competencies in adaptive instruction, mentorship, and the use of digital mastering tools. Creating supportive surroundings that encourage experimentation, reflection, and ongoing knowledge acquisition amongst educators is necessary for the profitable integration of customized learning.

Overcoming Resistance to Change: Resistance from educators, parents, and even college students can be a massive hurdle in the road toward personalized learning. Change can be daunting, and the shift from common instructional styles to customized methods is no exception. Addressing this mission requires a clear verbal exchange about the advantages of customized learning, showcasing success stories, and involving all stakeholders in the planning and implementation process. Building a way of life of trust, openness, and shared imagination and prescience can regularly alleviate resistance, paving the way for transformative exchange in education.

The challenges of customized learning, while substantial, are now not insurmountable. With considerate strategies, collaborative effort, and a relentless center of attention on the learner, the barriers can be overcome, bringing us closer to an academic paradigm where each and every scholar is empowered to attain their full potential. The options to these challenges are as varied as the freshmen they intend to serve, each contributing to the prosperous mosaic of personalized mastery in the digital age.

Real-World Examples of Personalized Learning

The theoretical underpinnings and technological improvements of customized mastering locate their authentic validation in the real-world contexts in which they are applied. Across the globe, numerous instructional settings have embraced personalized learning, adapting its ideas to their special occasions and demonstrating its transformative potential. These real-world examples now not solely illustrate the sensible utility of customized studying but additionally provide treasured insights into its effect on pupil engagement, achievement, and the broader academic ecosystem.

Elementary School in Silicon Valley: In a pioneering basic faculty nestled in the coronary heart of Silicon Valley, personalized knowledge acquisition is now not a future aspiration but an existing reality. Here, college students have interaction with a curriculum tailor-made to their man or woman, gaining knowledge of speeds, interests, and goals, facilitated with the aid of a modern adaptive getting-to-know platform. The platform tracks every student's development and adjusts the educational content material, accordingly, making sure that challenges are accurately scaled to the student's talent level. Teachers, free from the constraints of one-size-fits-all lesson plans, dedicate greater time to one-on-one instruction, deepening their appreciation of every student's needs. The end result is a bright knowledge of the neighborhood where college students show off greater ranges of engagement, confidence, and tutorial performance.

Rural High School in Scandinavia: Far from the tech hubs of the world, a rural excessive college in Scandinavia has converted its strategy to schooling by means of integrating personalized getting-to-know standards into its curriculum. Despite confined resources, the college leverages open-source applied sciences and a community-based method to create customized learning experiences for its students. Through project-based studying and a robust emphasis on self-directed study, college students discover their passions, guided by educators who act as mentors instead of common teachers. This method has no longer solely superior pupil motivation but has additionally fostered a tradition of innovation and independence, getting college students ready for the challenges of the twenty-first century.

Online University for Adult Learners: An online college catering to grownup beginners globally exemplifies the scalability of customized learning. By providing flexible, competency-based diploma programs, the college lets in college students develop at their personal pace, recognizing prior getting to know and expert experience. Adaptive evaluation applied sciences furnish on-the-spot feedback, tailoring the getting-to-know course to tackle man or woman strengths and weaknesses. This mannequin has enabled lots of grownup newbies to achieve their instructional goals, balancing their studies with expert and private responsibilities.

Public School District in an Urban Area: A giant public college district in a city location confronted with declining scholar engagement and fulfillment rankings became to personalized mastering as a method for reform. Implementing a district-wide customized program to gain knowledge of initiative, faculties had been geared up with digital equipment to help with individualized practice and real-time assessment. Professional improvement for instructors is targeted at fact literacy and differentiated training strategies. The initiative led to marked improvements in pupil performance, mainly in underserved communities, highlighting personalized learning's function in merchandising instructional equity.

International Baccalaureate School in Asia: At an International Baccalaureate (IB) college in Asia, personalized gaining knowledge is woven into the cloth of the curriculum, emphasizing inquiry-based gaining knowledge and international citizenship. Students engage in personalized initiatives that align with their pastimes and the IB's mission, utilizing digital portfolios to record their mastering journey. This strategy has cultivated a pupil physique that is no longer solely academically done but additionally deeply engaged with international issues, demonstrating the holistic influence of personalized learning.

These real-world examples of customized learning, spanning continents and academic contexts, underscore the versatility and have an effect on this approach. By tailoring training to meet the wants of character learners, faculties and establishments around the world are now not simply improving educational results but additionally nurturing a technology of newcomers geared up to navigate the complexities of the cutting-edge world. The training discovered from these examples furnishes a blueprint for others searching to embark on the ride of personalized learning, presenting hope and a course for the future of education.

Chapter 3: The Role of Artificial Intelligence in Education

Introduction to AI in Educational Contexts

The dawn of the twenty-first century has witnessed the emergence of synthetic genius (AI) as a transformative force throughout more than a few sectors, with training standing at the forefront of this technological renaissance. At its core, AI in training encapsulates the software of smart machines capable of performing duties that historically required human intelligence. These duties consist of grasping herbal language, recognizing patterns, fixing problems, and adapting to new information. This chapter introduces the vital principles of AI and explores its evolving position inside academic settings, marking a considerable shift in how getting to know is facilitated, managed, and assessed.

Evolution and Application: The experience of AI from a fledgling scientific self-discipline to a cornerstone of instructional innovation mirrors the speedy developments in computing strength and information analytics. Early functions of AI in schooling centered on fundamental duties such as programmed coaching and problem-solving drills. Today, however, AI's position has elevated exponentially, encompassing state-of-the-art adaptive learning systems, sensible tutoring systems, and computerized administrative tools. This evolution displays a broader grasp of AI's ability to cater to numerous getting-to-know needs, beautify pupil engagement, and streamline academic processes.

Key AI Concepts in Education: To recognize the effects of AI on education, it is essential to familiarize oneself with various underlying technologies. Machine learning, a subset of AI, permits structures to study data, become aware of patterns, and make choices with minimal human intervention. Natural language processing permits machines to apprehend and interpret human language, facilitating interactions between college students and AI-driven systems. Predictive analytics, like any other indispensable concept, makes use of historic information to make predictions about future events, helping in personalized mastery and early identification of college students who may also want extra support.

Transforming Teaching and Learning: The integration of AI in schooling guarantees a paradigm shift in educational methodologies and mastering experiences. Adaptive learning systems, powered via AI, tailor academic content material to the learner's pace, style, and preferences, providing a customized getting-to-know journey. For teachers, AI gives treasured insights into pupil performance, enabling focused interventions and support. Moreover, AI-driven equipment can automate time-consuming administrative tasks, permitting educators to focus extra on instructing and much less on paperwork.

Potential and Challenges: While the possibility of AI in training is vast, its profitable integration requires cautious consideration of a number of challenges, consisting of moral concerns, record privacy, and the digital divide. The stability of leveraging AI to beautify schooling while addressing these challenges is imperative to realizing its full potential.

As we embark on this exploration of AI's function in academic contexts, it becomes clear that we are standing on the cusp of a new generation in education. In this generation, the boundaries of what is feasible are consistently extended with the aid of the sensible software of technological know-how to create more effective, engaging, and inclusive getting-to-know environments. The trip of AI in training is now not simply about the science itself, but about reimagining the future of gaining knowledge in a world where human talent and synthetic genius converge to liberate unheard-of instructional opportunities.

AI-driven adaptive learning systems

The coronary heart of AI's transformative strength in schooling pulses most vigorously inside adaptive mastering systems. These state-of-the-art systems characterize the pinnacle of customized education, the place technological know-how and pedagogy intersect to create a getting-to-know journey that dynamically adjusts to the individual learner. This chapter delves into the mechanics, successes, and profound impact of AI-driven adaptive getting-to-know systems, supplying a glimpse into a future where schooling is now not simply tailor-made to the learner but evolves with them.

Mechanics of Adaptive Learning: At its core, adaptive learning makes use of a synthetic brain to analyze a student's interactions and overall performance in real-time, adjusting the difficulty, style, and pace of content material accordingly. This dynamic personalization is grounded in desktop studying algorithms that use giant quantities of records to perceive patterns in a student's studying behavior. By continually adapting to every learner's needs, these structures make certain that each pupil faces challenges that are neither too effortless nor too daunting, advertising the most appropriate getting-to-know stipulations for all.

Personalization at Scale: The genuine wonder of AI-driven adaptive learning lies in its capability to provide personalized mastering experiences at scale. In typical instructional settings, personalization is frequently restricted by the realistic constraints of teacher-to-student ratios. However, adaptive mastering structures spoil these boundaries, supplying individualized studying pathways to heaps or even heaps of college students simultaneously. This scalability ensures that the advantages of customized mastering are no longer a privilege for the few but are trendy for many.

Case Studies of Success: Across the globe, instructional establishments have begun to harness the electricity of adaptive mastering systems, witnessing amazing enhancements in scholar engagement and tutorial outcomes. For instance, a college enforcing an adaptive platform for its arithmetic guides discovered an enormous increase in ignoring charges and scholar satisfaction. Similarly, an excessive faculty using an adaptive software program for language arts noticed marked enhancements in analyzing comprehension and integral thinking capabilities amongst its students. These case studies no longer solely underscore the effectiveness of adaptive mastering structures, but additionally spotlight their workability to tackle academic challenges in various contexts.

Impact on Learner Engagement and Outcomes: Beyond educational achievement, AI-driven adaptive getting-to-know structures have a profound impact on scholar engagement. By imparting content material that aligns with every student's special hobbies and mastering preferences, these structures foster a deeper connection to the material, encouraging curiosity and a love for learning. The instant comments and attention supplied by using adaptive structures also encourage students, reinforcing their sense of development and achievement.

The exploration of AI-driven adaptive knowledge of structures displays a future where training is deeply personalized, quite engaging, and universally accessible. These structures now not solely venture the regular paradigms of instructing and mastering, but additionally open new avenues for academic fairness and excellence. As we proceed to unencumber the doable of synthetic brains in education, adaptive gaining knowledge of structures stands as a testimony to the strength of technological know-how to beautify human studying and creativity.

Automating administrative tasks for teachers

In the evolving panorama of academic technology, the synthetic brain (AI) emerges no longer solely as a facilitator of customized studying but additionally as an effective ally in streamlining administrative tasks. This chapter explores the widespread use of AI in automating the myriad administrative obligations that frequently devour educators' time, thereby enabling them to commit extra strength and focal point to the core mission of educating and guiding students.

Liberating Educators from Administrative Burdens: The administrative workload on instructors has long been a factor of concern, detracting from the time and interest that should, in any other case, be invested in scholar interplay and educational design. AI introduces a paradigm shift, automating hobbies duties such as attendance recording, grading of quizzes and assignments, and scheduling. By delegating these obligations to sensible systems, educators are afforded the freedom to interact more deeply with their students, customize gaining knowledge of experiences, and refine their teaching strategies.

Grading and Feedback Automation: One of the most time-consuming duties for educators, grading, is being revolutionized by using AI technologies. Intelligent algorithms can now precisely examine pupil responses to a huge variety of assignments, from multiple-choice questions to extra-complicated written work. Beyond mere grading, these structures can provide customized remarks to students, figuring out areas of power and suggesting sources for improvement. These immediate, data-driven comments help the studying process, fostering a responsive academic environment.

Efficiency in Scheduling and Resource Allocation: AI-driven equipment prolongs its utility to the logistical factors of education, such as classification scheduling and aid allocation. Intelligent structures can optimize schedules, taking into account the myriad variables that impact instructional programming, from trainer availability to pupil needs. This optimization now not only enhances the effectiveness of academic establishments but additionally contributes to a more cohesive getting-to-know journey for students.

The Broader Implications of Administrative AI: The automation of administrative duties by means of AI does more than simply alleviate the workload of educators; it signifies a broader transformation in the instructional landscape. With administrative responsibilities streamlined, establishments can reallocate resources in the direction of initiatives that at once influence scholar mastery and well-being. Furthermore, the statistics amassed via these automatic approaches provide precious insights into academic developments and outcomes, informing coverage and exercise at a systemic level.

The introduction of AI in automating administrative tasks inside schooling heralds a new generation of effectiveness in teaching. This technological empowerment of educators no longer solely enhances the fine art of schooling but additionally redefines the function of teachers, emphasizing their irreplaceable role as mentors, facilitators, and architects of the getting-to-know experience. As we navigate the future of education, the integration of AI in administrative domains stands as a beacon of progress, illuminating the route in the direction of an extra-focused, engaged, and human-centric method of educating and learning.

Ethical Considerations and Challenges of AI in Education

As synthetic genius (AI) weaves its problematic internet through the material of academic systems, it brings a mild spectrum of moral issues and challenges that demand our attention. The deployment of AI in training is now not basically a technical or pedagogical exercise but a deeply moral one, involving questions of privacy, equity, and the very nature of gaining knowledge of and teaching. This chapter delves into the moral panorama of AI in education, exploring the nuances of these challenges and proposing pathways to navigate them responsibly.

Navigating the Terrain of Data Privacy: At the coronary heart of AI-driven schooling lies the use of data—data that is personal, sensitive, and immensely powerful. The moral stewardship of this record is paramount, as it includes the belief and privateness of endless students. Educators and technologists have to tread this terrain with care, making sure that fact series and evaluation are carried out with the utmost respect for privacy and consent. This consists of obvious record policies, strong safety measures, and an unwavering dedication to the use of statistics in methods that benefit, rather than exploit, the learner.

Addressing Bias and Equity: Another vital moral task is the practicability of bias in AI algorithms and the broader implications for fairness in education. AI systems, with the aid of their very nature, examine current data, which can replicate historic biases and inequalities. Without cautious oversight, these biases can be perpetuated and amplified, leading to discriminatory outcomes. Ensuring that AI in schooling serves as a pressure for fairness requires a concerted effort to de-bias algorithms, diversify information sets, and always reveal unintended consequences.

The Impact on Teacher Roles: The integration of AI in training additionally raises questions about the evolving function of teachers. While AI can beautify and increase the instructional experience, there is a reputable situation that it should reduce the price positioned on human instructors or lead to a depersonalization of education. Navigating this task includes recognizing and reinforcing the irreplaceable features of human educators—qualities like empathy, moral judgment, and the capability to encourage and encourage college students in approaches that AI cannot.

Strategies for Ethical Implementation: Addressing the moral challenges of AI in training needs a multi-faceted strategy. This consists of creating moral tips for the use of AI in instructional settings, offering education for educators on the moral implications of AI, and involving various stakeholders in the improvement and deployment of AI technologies. Moreover, fostering an ongoing discussion about the moral dimensions of AI in schooling is essential for making sure that these applied sciences align with societal values and the common good.

The Way Forward: The moral issues and challenges of AI in schooling are complicated and multifaceted, reflecting the broader dilemmas that AI affords society. However, these challenges are now not insurmountable. By coming close to AI with a crucial and moral lens, educators, technologists, and policymakers can harness its potential while navigating its pitfalls. The purpose is to create an academic future that leverages AI to enhance learning, teaching, and administrative efficiency, all while upholding the best requirements of ethics, equity, and human dignity.

As we enter the age of synthetic intelligence, the moral concerns surrounding its use in training will continue to evolve. The route ahead requires vigilance, empathy, and a dedication to setting the human journey in the middle of technological advancement. By doing so, we can make certain that AI serves as a device for empowerment and enlightenment, rather than a supply of moral compromise.

Future Prospects of AI in Enhancing Learning

As we stand on the precipice of a new generation in education, formed with the aid of the relentless march of synthetic brains

(AI), it is exhilarating and crucial to ponder the future potentialities of AI in bettering learning. This remaining chapter casts its gaze forward, envisioning a future where AI no longer solely augments the instructional panorama but revolutionizes it, developing studying experiences that are more inclusive, engaging, and fantastic than ever before.

Emerging Technologies and Their Educational Potential: The future of AI in schooling is intrinsically linked to the development of rising technologies. Imagine digital truth (VR) environments where inexperienced people can immerse themselves in historic events, exploring historic civilizations as if taking walks through them. Consider augmented fact (AR) purposes that overlay academic content material onto the bodily world, remodeling mundane environments into shiny getting-to-know spaces. These technologies, powered by AI, keep the promise of making mastering now not simply interactive but clearly experiential.

Personalized Learning Taken to New Heights: The personalization abilities of AI are poised to turn out to be even more sophisticated, with algorithms that adapt now not simply to the educational stage of the student but also to their emotional country and getting to know their environment. Future AI structures ought to grant real-time changes to studying pathways that account for a student's mood, engagement level, and exterior distractions, making sure foremost getting to know stipulations at all times.

Assessment and Feedback Reimagined: The future additionally holds the potential for AI to radically change evaluation and comment mechanisms. Beyond automating grading, AI ought to provide deep insights into pupil understanding, figure out misconceptions, and master gaps with precision. This would allow educators to grant focused interventions and comments that are no longer solely well-timed but deeply personalized, aiding a greater nuanced grasp of every student's getting-to-know journey.

Enhancing Creativity and Problem-Solving: As AI takes on greater administrative and analytical tasks, educators will have increased freedom to center their attention on fostering creativity, imperative thinking, and problem-solving abilities amongst their students. Future academic AI should serve as a catalyst for creativity, supplying equipment and systems that inspire exploration, experimentation, and the advent of new knowledge.

Ethical and Equitable AI Deployment: Looking ahead, the moral deployment of AI in training will continue to be a paramount concern. The future will probably see the improvement of world requirements and moral frameworks that make certain AI is used responsibly, equitably, and in methods that decorate human dignity. These pointers will be fundamental in navigating the challenges of facts, privacy, bias, and the digital divide, making sure that the advantages of academic AI are handy to all learners, regardless of their background.

As we envision the future of AI in education, it is clear that its workability is as sizable as our collective imagination. The experience beforehand will require collaboration, innovation, and a steadfast dedication to the standards of fairness and ethics. Yet, the promise of AI to radically change education—to make it more personalized, engaging, and effective—offers a compelling imaginative and prescient vision of the future, one where each learner has the equipment and possibilities to attain their full potential.

In this future, AI in schooling transcends the position of a mere device or facilitator. It will become a companion in the mastering process, improving human abilities and opening new pathways for exploration and discovery. As we move forward, the integration of AI into training holds the promise of a renaissance in learning, a period of exceptional boom and innovation that will form the minds and hearts of future generations.

Chapter 4: Digital Literacy and Competencies

Characterizing Computerized Proficiency in the Twenty-First Hundred Years

In the embroidery of the 21st-century educational scene, computerized proficiency arises now not just as an ability but rather as an essential proficiency comparable in importance to perusing, composing, and math. This part opens by exploring the idea of computerized education, revealing insight into its significance in an age where science saturates every part of individual, scholastic, and master life. Computerized education rises above the crucial capacity to utilize programming projects or capability computerized gadgets; it envelops a total arrangement of capacities that permit individuals to get to, examine, make, and impart realities in an advanced climate.

The Critical Parts of Computerized Proficiency: At the coronary heart of advanced education lies a group of three quintessential parts: data education, mechanical expertise education, and media proficiency. Data proficiency furnishes individuals with the abilities to look at, assess, and use information successfully. Innovation proficiency involves appreciation for and utilization of computerized gadgets, applications, and organizations. Media proficiency expands this grip to the domain of media content, enabling individuals to analyze and connect with computerized media altogether. Together, these angles structure the premise of computerized education, empowering people to explore the advanced world with confidence and quintessential astuteness.

The Developing Idea of Computerized Proficiency: As advanced applied sciences continue to advance at an extraordinary speed, so too does the possibility of advanced education. What used to be a bunch of predominant capacities has now turned into a basic need for support in the computerized world. The meaning of computerized proficiency is dynamic, mirroring the relentless development of new advances, stages, and methods of correspondence. This development needs a devotion to deep-rooted realization, where computerized education capabilities are constantly evolving and modern because of the modifying computerized scene.

Understanding computerized proficiency in the twenty-first century requires a perception of its intricacy and its necessary capability to enable individuals to win in a carefully connected world. It is as of now not sufficient to be detached customers of computerized content; people must be dynamic, imperative members, fruitful at knowing the unwavering quality of data, getting a handle on the ramifications of computerized impressions, and adding to the computerized lodge in successful and huge ways.

As we dig further into the subtleties of computerized proficiency, obviously encouraging this ability is essential for preparing undergrads for what's in store. Instructors, policymakers, and networks need to work together to ensure that computerized proficiency preparation is open, extensive, and aligned with the desires of a quickly changing world. Thusly, we can deliver the maximum capacity of computerized applied sciences to enhance learning, cultivate development, and make people more proficient and drawn to the public eye.

Fundamental Computerized Abilities for Understudies and Instructors

In the computerized age, the authority of advanced abilities is central for every understudy and teacher, molding not exclusively their instructional exercise achievement but rather furthermore their ability to flourish in a startlingly developing world. This section dives into the computerized capabilities that are essential in the twenty-first century, providing a guide for coordinating these abilities into the scholarly experience of newbies and the master improvement of educators.

Center for Computerized Abilities for the Twenty-First Hundred Years: At the coronary heart of basic computerized skills lies a huge number of possibilities that range from key computerized proficiency—for example, exploring web conditions and valuing advanced insurance and security—to extra-prevalent capabilities like advanced content material creation, insight examination, and coding. These capacities permit understudies to communicate with computerized content material harshly and imaginatively, clear up issues, and talk effectively within the scope of computerized designs. For instructors, the authority of computerized gear for training and learning, as well as the capacity to illuminate undergrads about their advanced abilities, is similarly essential.

Methodologies for Coordinating Computerized Abilities Preparing: Installing advanced abilities into the educational program requires a conscious and organized approach. This comprises planning illustration designs that contain advanced apparatuses, creating tasks that move the utilization of computerized assets, and utilizing project-based figuring out how to acquire information on the obligation's undergrads have in fixing certifiable issues with the use of innovation. For instructors, master improvement bundles focused on state-of-the art advanced schooling hardware and procedures are fundamental, offering them the abilities and confidence to actually incorporate innovative skills into their educational rehearsals.

The Job of Instructors in Demonstrating and Showing Computerized Proficiency: Teachers assume an essential part in training computerized education, never again exclusively through conferring, but rather through displaying responsible and decent advanced conduct. This incorporates showing how to think about the believability of online sources, engage in conscious advanced correspondence, and explore the ethical situations that happen in computerized spaces. By encapsulating these practices, teachers can impart to undergrads a familiarity with advanced commitment, accentuating the meaning of quintessential reasoning, sympathy, and moral propensities on the web.

The development of computerized capacities in undergrads and teachers is, as of now, not just a scholastic but a cultural need. In this present reality where computerized applied sciences are pivotal to every single component of everyday life, these capacities are major for private strengthening, urban commitment, and expert availability. The excursion to advanced capability is continuous, upsetting, relentless, acquiring information on and transformation. In any case, by focusing on the improvement of these crucial advanced abilities, educational foundations can now assemble understudies and teachers not just to explore the computerized world but also to frame it.

Incorporating computerized education across the educational plan

The pivotal job of meshing computerized proficiency consistently into the material of preparation requires a technique that rises above common concern limits, implanting these important capabilities all through the educational plan. This joining guarantees that computerized proficiency is presently not a distant region but rather an unavoidable piece of the educational experience, furnishing understudies with the benefit they need to flourish in a carefully interconnected world.

Best Practices for Implanting Computerized Education: Effective joining of computerized proficiency requires an intentional arrangement of curricular objectives with computerized skills, ensuring that understudies now not exclusively look at advanced hardware but rather furthermore practice them harshly and inventively all through situational regions. This can be achieved through cooperative undertakings that persuade understudies to explore, make, and talk about the utilization of advanced innovations, as well as using computerized structures that work with intuitive concentration on encounters.

Interdisciplinary Ventures and Exercises: The energy of inter-disciplinary errands lies in their capacity to mirror the intricacy of certifiable difficulties, irritating a combination of content data and computerized abilities. For example, an endeavor that joins science, innovation, designing, and math (STEM) themes with computerized narrating can require understudies to accumulate and examine data on a close-by ecological issue, then utilize computerized hardware to make a powerful interactive media show upholding neighborhood activity. Such errands now not exclusively brighten computerized education but rather furthermore cultivate fundamental reasoning, cooperation, and verbal trade abilities.

Decisive Reasoning and Moral Contemplations: Incorporat-ing computerized proficiency all through the educational program furthermore incorporates developing a vital and moral demeanor toward mechanical skill use. This comprises teaching undergrads to essentially think about the dependability and predisposition of advanced content, perceive the ramifications of computerized impressions, and explore the ethical quandaries presented through computerized innovations. By inserting these issues into all worry regions, instructors can verify that undergrads have a nuanced view of the computerized world and their area inside it.

The combination of computerized education throughout the educational plan is presently not just a scholastic methodology but instead a basic reaction to the requirements of the twenty-first century. It recognizes that computerized benefits are basic, never again just for instructive achievement but for full support in the public eye. By implanting computerized proficiency in every part of training, schools can assemble undergrads to explore the intricacies of the advanced age with certainty, imagination, and a key eye. This comprehensive technique guarantees that computerized education is presently not just an extra, but a center element of the dominant excursion, essential to improving balanced, informed, and drawn-in residents.

Defeating hindrances to advanced proficiency

The way to customary computerized proficiency is flung with im-pediments, from the advanced gap to opposition towards the com-bination of mechanical skill in training. These hindrances, whenever left ignored, take steps to broaden scholastic disparities and smother the opportunities for advancement and development. This part dives into the difficulties that impede the improvement of advanced education and investigates strategies for defeating them, ensuring that the benefits of computerized tutoring are accessible to all.

Defying the Computerized Separation: The advanced gap, the opening between these with a right of passage to computerized ap-plied sciences and these without, remains an aggressive hindrance to advanced education. This gap is presently not just about substantial access to gadgets and the web; it also encompasses advancements in advanced capabilities and information. To close this gap, purposeful endeavors are needed from states, scholarly foundations, and the non-public sector. Drives, for example, providing minimal-cost web access, putting resources into a computerized framework, and sending off local area-based training applications can play a crucial role in evening out the computerized diversion field.

Addressing the Absence of Admittance to Innovation: The absence of admittance to science in underserved networks and low-paying families represents an extraordinary test for achieving computerized proficiency. Systems to handle this issue comprise forcing mechanical ability loaning programs so the spot undergrads can get contraptions for homegrown use and collaborating with neighborhood gatherings and libraries to supply area access to advanced assets. Also, insurance contracts that guide the allotment of cash for science by joining in resources can verify that scholastic foundations are equipped with the quintessential advanced devices.

Handling Protection from innovation Joining: Protection from the reconciliation of computerized applied sciences in training, whether from teachers, guardians, or policymakers, can forestall endeavors to advance computerized proficiency. Beating this opposition requires clear verbal communication about the upsides of computerized education, never again exclusively for individual satisfaction but also for cultural progression. Proficient improvement applications that furnish teachers with the capacities and self-conviction to join science into their guidance can furthermore mitigate fears, as can including father and mother and neighborhood givers in computerized education drives to encourage a strong climate.

Imaginative Instructive Models to Help Advanced Proficiency: Tending to the limits of computerized education also involves reexamining scholarly styles to more readily help the improvement of advanced abilities. This might incorporate embracing mixed getting-to-know systems that blend normal and computerized guidance, developing creator regions that rouse involved dominating with innovation, and coordinating undertaking-based dominating that stresses the utilization of advanced hardware to cure genuine issues.

The ride towards huge computerized proficiency is full of difficulties; in any case, it is also packed with opportunities for extraordinary change. By addressing the limits that deter admittance to and commitment to computerized advances, society can deliver the possibility of advanced tutoring to enable people, span imbalances, and encourage a comprehensive and learned world. The procedures framed in this part outfit a diagram for beating these snags, preparing for a future where computerized education is presently not an honor but rather a right accessible to all.

Projects and Drives Advancing Computerized Proficiency

The mission to pervade computerized proficiency all through the range of society is, as of now, not a lone outing but rather an aggregate undertaking, set apart by the commitments of various applications and drives that have enlightened the course forward. This part praises these spearheading endeavors, investigating a scope of beneficial applications and drives that have taken gigantic steps in advancing computerized education at neighborhood, public, and overall levels. Through an assessment of what makes these applications compelling, this segment manages the cost of experiences in future directions for scaling and further developing computerized proficiency drives to meet the desires of a different and advancing total populace.

Focus on Effective Projects: All over the planet, current bundles have arisen, each with its own unique procedure for cultivating advanced education. For instance, expansive drives that supply computerized units and net admission to universities in underserved networks play a crucial role in evening out the scholarly happiness field. Non-benefit organizations granting after-school coding and computerized capabilities to studios have lit a fervor for mechanical skills among more youthful students. Also, public libraries have reexamined themselves as center points for computerized proficiency, providing free access to advanced resources and instructing bundles for all ages.

Key Variables for Progress: The investigation of these beneficial drives shows various regular components that add to their adequacy. Right off the bat, partner commitment, including teachers, guardians, understudies, and neighborhood individuals, guarantees that bundles are tailor-made to the specific needs and settings of their crowds. Furthermore, adaptable and versatile educational plans empower the reconciliation of advanced applied sciences and instructive techniques. At last, progressing assessment and input instruments are fundamental for estimating the impact of advanced education drives and making iterative enhancements.

Cooperation Across Areas: The improvement of computerized proficiency requires deliberate endeavors not only from educational foundations but also from power bodies, non-public area elements, and non-benefit associations. Organizations between these areas can supply the fundamental assets, mastery, and direction expected to scale computerized proficiency bundles. For example, specialists' insurance contracts that boost non-public quarter financing in computerized preparation can prod advancement and grow the achievement of advanced education drives.

Future Headings for Computerized Proficiency Drives: As we are, by all accounts, going into the future, obviously, computerized education drives need to develop to keep up with mechanical headways. This comprises expanding the extent of computerized proficiency to typify rising regions like engineered knowledge, network protection, and measurement morals. Besides, there is a growing desire to verify that computerized proficiency bundles are comprehensive, tending to the cravings of different students, incorporating those with inabilities, non-local speakers, and more established adults.

All in all, the bundles and drives featured in this section mean guides to advancement in the journey of laid-out computerized education. Their victories highlight the potential for advanced preparation to engage people, improve lives, and extend separation. As we push ahead, the directions found from these drives can illuminate improvements regarding new procedures and joint efforts, ensuring that the computerized age is an innovation of plausibility and inclusivity for all. Through aggregate movement and development, we can grow the skylines of computerized education, preparing for a future where every individual has the capacity and expertise to explore the computerized world unhesitatingly and capably.

Chapter 5: Overcoming Obstacles in Digital Education

Tending to the computerized partition

In the journey to saddle the maximum capacity of computerized schooling, the advanced gap looms as a striking obstruction, depicting at this point not just a mechanical opening but rather a gorge of chance. This separation, portrayed by inconsistent admittance to computerized applied sciences and the web, creates an extended shaded area over the commitment of computerized instruction, taking steps to leave at the rear of these on the mistaken feature of the gap. This region digs into the multi-layered nature of the advanced gap, investigating its suggestions for rookies and framing deliberate procedures to overcome this issue, accordingly democratizing admittance to computerized learning.

The Degree and Effect of the Computerized Gap: The advanced separation influences networks around the world, changing in seriousness from city regions, where fast web might be unreasonably expensive, to distant regions, where networks are a unique case. This separation now obstructs access to computerized learning resources as well as further compounds current educational disparities, restricting the opportunities for people to reinforce the advanced abilities crucial for support in the contemporary economy. The repercussions of this separation stretch out past the homeroom, affecting future work prospects and broadening financial differences.

Techniques for Overcoming Any Issues: Conquering the computerized partition needs a multi-layered approach, captivating specialists, scholarly organizations, non-benefits, and the non-public area in an aggregate effort. Framework improvement drives that draw out broadband access to underserved regions are essential. Similarly essential are applications that supply economical devices to understudies and instructors, ensuring that equipment is presently not an obstruction to computerized learning. Local area commitment assumes an urgent role, with libraries, neighborhood focuses, and resources proceeding as get-right-to-section factors for computerized learning, specifically in networks where the homegrown net get-right-to-passage is restricted.

Featuring Effective Drives: Across the globe, moderate drives uncover how coordinated exertion and cooperation can be managed. For instance, a few regions have completed cell-net gadgets that pass availability on to distant regions, empowering undergrads to get the right of section to computerized dominating stages. Public-private associations have come about with a supported broadband get-option to proceed for low-paying families, ensuring that financial requirements never again deflect advanced training. Such drives never again exclusively span the computerized partition, but rather act as a declaration of the power of aggregate movement in conquering restrictions in computerized training.

Tending to the computerized partition is presently not just a specialized venture but additionally a moral goal, key to the innovative and insightful quest for fair access to training. By recognizing the extent of this difficulty and forcing key arrangements, society can draw nearer to where every student, no matter what their geological or financial status, has the right of section to the potential outcomes managed by advanced training. This endeavor is imperative for building a comprehensive, informed, and connected world where the extraordinary feasibility of computerized dominance is reachable to all.

Guaranteeing Availability for All Students

In the mosaic of computerized schooling, ensuring openness for all students remains a declaration of the norms of decency and inclusivity. This section dives into the essential meaning of making computerized preparing resources reachable to understudies with handicaps, unwinding the intricacies, and giving choices that guarantee a concentrating on climate in which no student is abandoned.

The Basics of Openness: Availability in computerized preparation is currently not just a jail command or an ethical commitment; the foundation of an educational gadget esteems every single student's true capacity. It incorporates computerized content material and designs that are usable for undergrads with a gigantic assortment of handicaps, comprising of visual, hear-able, engine, and mental impedances. This devotion to openness guarantees that all understudies have equivalent chances to learn, connect with, and find true success in the computerized domain.

Best Practices for Making Comprehensive Computerized Content: Accomplishing openness in advanced preparation expects adherence to acceptable practices and norms, for example, the Internet Content Availability Rules (WCAG). These practices include providing text-based content picks for non-text content, ensuring content material can be explored and grasped without vision, and making all presentations convenient through a console. Also, utilizing reachable arrangement principles never again exclusively benefits understudies with incapacities; however, it improves the reading experience for all undergrads by bestowing more than one expertise of commitment and articulation.

Utilizing Innovation to Advance Availability: Current science presents unfathomable conceivable outcomes to enhance openness in schooling. Screen perusers, discourse-to-message applications, and flexible show settings are just a couple of instances of how mechanical skill can oblige different dominant requirements. Further, informative frameworks that contain man-made intelligence and processing gadgets can adjust to individual student inclinations and prerequisites, introducing customized availability inclinations that were once incomprehensible.

Contextual Investigations of Compelling Execution: Across the globe, scholarly foundations are spearheading current techniques for helpful advanced learning. From colleges that have completely implicit availability viewpoints into their web-based distributions to K–12 resources that outfit total assistive science helps for under-studies, these contextual investigations enlighten the course forward. They uncover that with legitimate responsibility, assets, and pro-cedures, advanced tutoring can be a viable motor for inclusivity.

The Excursion Ahead: As we work on as well as enter the com-puterized age, the mission for convenient advanced preparation stays continuous. It currently needs not exclusively constant mechanical development but rather, moreover, a social change in the course of perceiving and esteeming ranges of abilities to dominate. By supporting openness, teachers, policymakers, and technologists can work by and large to destroy the limits that keep understudies with handicaps from accomplishing their maximum capacity, proclaim-ing a future where computerized preparation is, as a general rule, for everybody.

Guaranteeing openness for all first-year recruits in computerized tutoring is a diverse errand that encompasses specialized, educa-tional, and moral aspects. However, it is also a significant chance to rethink tutoring as a generally helpful pathway to strengthening, information, and opportunity. As this part finishes up, it becomes apparent that the ride to convenient computerized tutoring is currently not just about beating hindrances but rather about building extensions to a comprehensive and fair future.

Adjusting screen time and wellbeing

In the advanced period, where showcases are the home windows to information, stresses over the impact of unnecessary presentation screen time on wellbeing have arisen as large difficulties to computerized schooling. This part explores the refined dependability between outfitting the benefits of advanced considering and shielding the substantial and scholarly prosperity of understudies. It highlights the meaning of obliging commitment with computerized gadgets, conferring bits of knowledge and methods to consolidate screen time into educational practices without compromising wellbeing.

Understanding the Effect of Screen Time: Inordinate showcase screen time is connected with an assortment of wellness worries, from eye pressure and rest unsettling influences to diminished substantially distraction and its orderly dangers. In children and youths, expanded exposure can also affect scholarly wellbeing, adding to feelings of disengagement or nervousness. Perceiving these impacts is the most vital move towards creating methods that moderate risks while utilizing the gifts of advanced learning devices.

Procedures for Solid Screen Commitment: To check the achievable awful aftereffects of show time, instructors, moms, and dads can utilize incalculable methodologies. These comprise executing typical presentation screen breaks eventually of computerized concentrating on meetings, empowering in essence exercises, and promoting exact ergonomics to prevent eye pressure and outer muscle issues. Also, coordinating clear tips for show use beyond scholarly activities can assist with controlling widespread presentation screen openness.

Incorporating Active Work and Health: Coordinating material amusement into the advanced preparation system is essential to adjusting show time. This can be done through integrating movement breaks into the school day, the utilization of exuberant getting-to-know systems that require in essence commitment, and introducing hotspots for undergrads to collaborate in substantial activities at home. Health rehearses, like care gym routine schedules and stress organization methods, can furthermore be incorporated into computerized stages, giving undergrads hardware to control their prosperity in a comprehensive way.

Instructive Strategies and Screen Using time productively: Creating and upholding scholastic insurance contracts that tackle show screen time organization is indispensable to fostering a sound computerized focus on climate. These insurance contracts should comprise ideas for day-to-day show screen time restrictions all through staff hours, pointers for gadget-free periods, and the advancement of the option of non-screen-based concentration on exercises. By putting together a system that focuses on wellbeing, scholastic foundations can encourage a lifestyle of cognizant presentation use.

The Way Ahead: Adjusting show screen time and wellness in computerized preparation requires a cooperative effort among teachers, guardians, policymakers, and understudies themselves. It incorporates now not exclusively putting limits and giving inclinations to screen-based activities, yet moreover showing all partners the meaning of balance and the feasible wellness ramifications of computerized framework use. As advanced preparing keeps on developing, so should our strategies for overseeing show screen time, ensuring that the computerized upheaval in preparing upgrades as opposed to reducing researcher prosperity.

All in all, the excursion towards a decent connection with screen time in tutoring is muddled and multi-layered. However, by taking on a proactive and educated approach, it is feasible to explore this computerized display such that jelly wellness and prosperity while embracing the colossal scholastic prospects that innovative skill gives.

Shielding protection and information security

In the advanced preparation scene, where sizable amounts of researcher realities are gathered, dissected, and put away, the need to safeguard security and make specific measurements safeguarded has not the slightest bit been more basic. This section digs into the confounded web of difficulties connected with protecting sensitive realities in an educational setting, illustrating procedures to maintain the least demanding prerequisites of protection and security.

The Meaning of Protection and Information Security: The computerized age has introduced unmatched opportunities for customized learning and information-driven scholastic systems. Nonetheless, these advancements accompany the obligation to guard the security of understudies and the wellbeing of their information. Breaks in privateness and factual security now not exclusively subvert understudies' trust in scholastic foundations but rather also present immense threats to understudies' security and prosperity.

Lawful Systems and Best Works on: Exploring the display of security and measurement wellbeing requires an exhaustive enthusiasm for criminal structures, for example, the Family Instructive Freedoms and Protection Act (FERPA) in the US, the Overall Information Assurance Guideline (GDPR) in the European Association, and different provincial and extensive guidelines. These legitimate rules give a premise to top-of-the line rehearses in data taking care of, alongside thoughts of record minimization, assent, straightforwardness, and responsibility. Sticking to these criminal necessities guarantees that educational applied sciences are utilized in approaches that value protection privileges and gatekeeper delicate data.

Carrying out Powerful Safety Efforts: To protect information, educational foundations and innovative skills merchants ought to place into areas of strength for impact measures. This comprises the utilization of encryption to safeguard measurements on the way and very still, ordinary assurance reviews to see weaknesses, and the improvement of episode reaction intends to handle reachable reality breaks. Teaching undergrads and the labor force about network safety rehearsals, for example, solid passwords and comprehension of phishing assaults, comparably reinforces the security stance of educational conditions.

Instructing the Instructive People Group: A fundamental issue for defending security and record wellbeing is training. Understudies, teachers, and chairmen should be proficient about the meaning of measurements and security, the risks connected with advanced innovations, and the means they can take to monitor private data. Studios, training meetings, and continuous discussions about protection and security can cultivate a way of life of cautiousness and obligation.

The Way Ahead: As science keeps on developing, so will the difficulties of protection and information wellbeing in advanced schooling. The course ahead requires a proactive and cooperative methodology, including policymakers, teachers, mechanical skill suppliers, and the more extensive local area. By remaining educated about rising dangers, taking on extraordinary practices in reality, and pushing for powerful security assurances, the educational locale can explore the intricacies of the computerized age while defending the privileges and assurances of students.

Taking everything into account, devotion to protection and data wellbeing is essential to the uprightness and progress of advanced schooling. By tending to these difficulties head-on, teachers and foundations can now not exclusively monitor tricky keeps yet moreover build confidence and confidence in the computerized world, acquiring information on the climate and ensuring that it remains a protected, comprehensive, and enabling house for all understudies.

Procedures for Viable Execution of Computerized Instruments

The reception and combination of advanced hardware in preparation describe a huge change in educational work, promising to upgrade growth opportunities and results. Be that as it may, this progress is no longer without its difficulties. This section investigates the multi-layered restrictions that teachers and foundations face in upholding computerized hardware effectively and frames vital cycles to conquer these hindrances, consequently expanding the reachable science to truly change training.

Recognizing Normal Obstructions: The fine joining of computerized hardware into scholastic settings is much of the time prevented by a scope of variables, which incorporate limited innovative foundation, protection from substitute among instructors and chairmen, and an absence of schooling and backing. Also, the quick rhythm of mechanical advancement can leave teachers battling to stay aware of new hardware and techniques, certainly prompting underutilization or insufficient utility of science in the study hall.

The Job of an Educator: Preparing and Proficient Turn of events: Fundamental to conquering these difficulties is the arrangement of complete teacher schooling and master improvement, which are valuable open doors. Instructors should now be equipped not exclusively with the specialized abilities to use advanced gear but also with the academic discernment to integrate them into their education. This comprises training on the best way to utilize mechanical ability to work with fiery learning, separate guidance, and actually take a look at understudy dominance in moderate ways. Consistent master improvement potential open doors, comprehensive of studios, workshops, and online courses, can assist teachers with staying side by side of cutting-edge computerized hardware and scholarly techniques.

Assessing and Choosing Advanced Apparatuses: With the plenty of computerized hardware accessible, picking the most breathtaking, applied sciences for informative capabilities can dismay. Establishments and teachers ought to embrace a precise technique for assessing computerized devices, pondering components like arrangement with curricular objectives, convenience, openness, and confirmation of viability. Including teachers in the decision-making process guarantees that the picked hardware meets the genuine cravings of educators and students, encouraging an encounter of ownership and commitment to the beneficial coordination of innovation.

Conquering Protection from Change: Protection from the reception of computerized gear can consistently originate from an absence of an impression of its practicable benefits or from worry about the difficulties of coordinating science into current instructive structures. Tending to this obstruction requires clear verbal trade about the job of advanced hardware in further developing learning, as well as the arrangement of help structures, for example, tutoring and peer help organizations, to assist teachers with exploring the change.

The Way to Computerized Combination: The beneficial execution of computerized hardware in tutoring is an excursion that requires careful preparation, progressing support, and a readiness to incorporate change. It remembers fostering a lifestyle of development in which instructors are invigorated to examine new innovations, reproduce their practices, and offer their encounters with partners. By taking on a cooperative, vital way to deal with the coordination of computerized devices, educational foundations can defeat the limits that substitute the method of mechanical change, opening new probabilities for teaching and dominating in the computerized age.

All in all, the great execution of computerized gear in tutoring is a confounded, however feasible, objective. Through focused preparation and accommodating correlation of innovations and procedures to help change, teachers and foundations can harness the power of computerized gear to make connecting with, dynamic, and positive concentrating on conditions. As this part closes, obviously the eventual fate of preparing is advanced, and by embracing this future with aim and care, we can ensure that it is also brilliant.

Conclusion: Envisioning the Future of Education

Summing up Key Bits of Knowledge from the Computerized Learning Insurgency

As we stand at the conjunction of culture and development in schooling, it is essential to consider the experience embraced through the advanced, dominant upheaval. This groundbreaking development, set apart through the combination of advanced applied sciences into the educational texture, has reshaped the display of getting to be aware and teaching in significant ways. The experience has been one of variation, challenge, and an incredible open door, yielding bits of knowledge that will illuminate the future regarding schooling.

The Groundbreaking Effect of Computerized Advancements: The computerized acquisition of information has introduced an excellent option in schooling. Advancements like engineered insight, versatile dominating stages, and computerized education gear have now not exclusively sped up the section on tutoring but rather altered the dominating experience. This change has empowered tenderfoots to cooperate with content material all the more profoundly, at their own speed, and in manners that line up with their male or female concentrating on styles.

Shift Towards Customized and Versatile Learning: One of the vastest experiences from the advanced getting-to-realize upset is the shift toward altered learning. Computerized applied sciences have made it possible to fit informative substance material to meet the unique needs of each and every understudy, recognizing that getting to know is currently not a one-size-fits-all interaction. Versatile dominating frameworks, controlled by computer-based intelligence, have taken this personalization as well as powerfully acclimating to the student's advancement, conferring difficulties, and supporting precisely when they are required.

Combination of Computerized Education: The transformation has furthermore highlighted the meaning of computerized proficiency as a crucial capacity in the twenty-first century. As computerized hardware becomes irreplaceable to learning, the ability to explore, assess, and make advanced content material has become imperative for undergrads and teachers alike. The reconciliation of computerized proficiency all through educational programs addresses a commitment to preparing novices for an advanced world, furnishing them with the capacities to find true success academically, expertly, and by and by.

Exploring Difficulties and Observing Accomplishments: The advanced insurgency has not been without challenges. Issues such as advanced separation, protection concerns, and the longing for even-handed admittance to mechanical skill have featured regions where supported exertion and development are important. However, the accomplishments—upgraded commitment, expanded openness, and the democratization of training—offer a convincing declaration of the transformation's brilliant effect.

As we sum up the vital experiences from the advanced concentrating on transformation, obviously this excursion has changed not just the way in which we advance but also how we expect about preparing itself. It has opened up new probabilities for commitment, openness, and personalization, making way for a future where preparing is extra comprehensive, versatile, and lined up with the needs of a startlingly changing world. The preparation acknowledged through this upheaval will proceed to empower and provide data as we explore the developing display of computerized training.

Proceeding with the Development of Instructive Advances

As we look forward, the skyline of educational applied sciences extends limitlessly, promising a future where dominance is persistently changed and improved with the guidance of development. The advanced, dominant upheaval, while pivotal, addresses just the foundation of a continuous excursion. This section investigates the tireless rhythm of the mechanical turn of events and its capability to change the scholarly scene, giving a brief look into the propensities and hardware that will shape the eventual fate of advancing in much the same way.

Expecting Future Patterns in Computerized Training: The discipline of educational mechanical skill is dynamic, with new improvements ascending at a stunning speed. Counterfeit Virtuoso (man-made intelligence), advanced fact (VR), increased reality (AR), and blockchain are at the very front of these turns of events, each providing unique probabilities for improving getting to know encounters. Man-made intelligence's prescient capacities vow to make modified acquiring of information significantly more nuanced, while VR and AR can allow vivid acquiring of information on conditions that rise above substantial limits. Blockchain innovation, with its true capacity for firmly shutting and clear credentialing, may change how scholarly accomplishments are recorded and perceived.

Arising Innovations Forming Learning and Educating: The reconciliation of rising applied sciences into tutoring is presently not just about embracing new gear but also about reconsidering the actual idea of guidance and learning. For example, computer-based intelligence-driven examination ought to furnish teachers with profound experiences in understudies acquiring information on designs, empowering more noteworthy invaluable assistance and intercession. All the while, improvements in natural language handling should make computerized collaborators a fundamental part of the concentrating on process, bestowing understudies practice and resources progressively.

The Potential for More Notable Personalization and Commitment: As educational applied sciences develop, so too does the usefulness of concentrating on encounters that are profoundly altered and locked in. Future applied sciences should now adjust not exclusively to the instructive level of the student but furthermore to their sentiments and inspiration, growing information on environmental elements that answers the comprehensive needs of the student. This level of personalization can possibly build commitment, inspiration, and, at last, authority over results.

Planning for an Eventual Fate of Constant Development: The diligence of the development of informative applied sciences requires a way of life of relentless learning and transformation among teachers and undergrads alike. It expects teachers to be deep-rooted students, persistently refreshing their capacities and instructive strategies to actually use new applied sciences. For understudies, it underlines the meaning of versatility and flexibility, preparing them for a future where trade is the sole consistent.

As we imagine the eventual fate of training, obviously the experience of carefully acquiring information is some distance from complete. The persistence of the advancement of educational applied sciences presents each commitment and challenge, expecting us to constantly rethink the probabilities of learning. By embracing development and encouraging a practice of constant learning, we can ensure that the fate of preparing is one where every single student gets the opportunity to achieve their maximum capacity in a consistently impacting world.

Planning for the Difficulties Ahead

As we explore the consistently advancing scene of computerized instruction, it becomes fundamental to expect and get ready for the difficulties that lie ahead. The experience of working with a completely inherent computerized contraption is full of intricacies that require foreknowledge, versatility, and a commitment to reasonableness and greatness. This section investigates the feasible limits throughout advanced schooling's future and diagrams key strategies to defeat them, ensuring that the computerized getting to realize upheaval keeps on advantaging all students.

Distinguishing Future Difficulties: The fast rhythm of mechanical headway, while giving titanic open doors, furthermore manages the cost of boundless difficulties. These comprise ensuring fair access to innovation, defending measurable protection and security, and holding humans to account for tutoring in the midst of developing mechanization. Also, the longing for relentless master improvement for teachers to hold rhythm with new applied sciences arises as a fundamental test, requiring foundational direction and assets.

Methodologies for Tending to Value and Access: To ensure that the advanced tutoring upset helps every single understudy, designated endeavors should be made to connect the computerized partition. This incorporates never again exclusively introducing the right of passage to devices and the rapid web, but also ensuring that advanced substance material is socially responsive and accessible to understudies with incapacities. Public-private organizations, local area-based drives, and focused inclusion mediations can play a crucial role in expanding access to and encouraging a comprehensive computerized dominating climate.

Shielding Information Protection and Security: As computerized preparation turns out to be progressively information-driven, safeguarding researcher security and getting educational realities against breaks develop to be principal concerns. Taking on strong network protection measures, making clear measurement and administration arrangements, and showing undergrads and teachers advanced security rehearsals are basic moves toward developing an impenetrable computerized preparation environment.

Keeping up with the Human Component: In the midst of the joining of computer-based intelligence, robotization, and different applied sciences in schooling, protecting the human component—underscoring compassion, moral thinking, and relational associations—stays essential. Teachers play an indispensable role in concentrating on encounters that encourage social-close-to-home turns of events, significant reasoning, and imagination. Offsetting mechanical combinations with the support of these human-driven capacities is critical to preparing understudies for a mind-boggling, interconnected world.

Nonstop Expert Advancement for Teachers: Furnishing instructors with the abilities and understanding to accurately consolidate computerized applied sciences into educating and getting to know is a continuous test. Putting resources into complete master improvement programs, creating networks of training, and bestowing teachers with the right of passage to the present-day scholastic applied sciences and educational procedures are principals for cultivating a moderately and responsively informative labor force.

As we plan ahead for computerized schooling, obviously the heading is both promising and testing. By proactively tending to the obstacles of value, access, security, and the assurance of the human issue in schooling, we can verify that the advanced concentrating on upheaval keeps on unfurling in techniques that are comprehensive, secure, and profoundly human. Getting ready for these moves requires an aggregate devotion to development, value, and constant picking up, preparing for a future where computerized preparing enables every single student to accomplish their ideal potential.

The Job of Strategy and Administration in Forming What's in store

As the computerized preparation scene proceeds to enhance and advance, the significance of visionary administration and strong inclusion structures couldn't possibly be more significant. These variables are fundamental in exploring the intricacies of coordinating science into scholastic practices and ensuring that the advanced getting-to-realize transformation helps all citizens. This part dives into the vital role that inclusion and the board play in encouraging development and directing the scholastic zone through the difficulties and potential outcomes presented by advanced advancements.

Visionary Initiative for a Computerized Age: At the coronary heart of beneficial computerized tutoring drives lies a board that is both visionary and logical. Pioneers in training, whether at the level of individual foundations or inside more extensive scholarly frameworks, need to have a profound grasp of the conceivable utilization of computerized applied sciences to enhance learning. They ought to also have the foreknowledge to anticipate future propensities and the difficulties they may, in addition, present. Successful administration in computerized tutoring involves supporting development, cultivating a custom of relentless learning and transformation, and ensuring that educational practices are lined up with the advancing cravings of undergrads in an advanced world.

Steady Strategies for Supportable Advancement: The improvement and execution of ground-breaking insurance contracts are key to growing a climate in which computerized tutoring can flourish. These insurance contracts need to handle key regions like subsidizing for innovative skill foundation, master improvement for teachers, educational plan improvement that comprises computerized proficiency and abilities, and prerequisites for reality, protection, and security. Furthermore, insurance contracts should be intended to advance reasonableness and access, ensuring that no researcher is abandoned in the change to computerized training. By introducing a reasonable system and guide for development, inclusion can prepare for scholastic practices that are present-day, comprehensive, and viable.

Joint effort Between Partners: The molding representing things to come of preparing in the computerized age requires cooperation among an enormous range of partners, including teachers, policymakers, science suppliers, understudies, and guardians. This cooperative methodology guarantees that various perspectives and information are conveyed to understudies on the difficulties and conceivable outcomes of computerized training. It also permits the sharing of excellent practices, the improvement of associations, and the co-production of choices that are receptive to longings, everything being equal.

The Significance of Value and Inclusivity in Approach and Administration: As advanced tutoring keeps on developing, ensuring that decency and inclusivity stay at the forefront of inclusion and board decisions is fundamental. This limit is effectively attempting to eliminate snags to get to, address the advanced gap, and gain information on conditions that appreciate and oblige assortment in the entirety of its structures. Approaches and board methods that focus on decency can assist with verifying that the benefits of computerized tutoring are generally shared and that all understudies have the likelihood of succeeding.

All in all, the elements of inclusion and the board in forming the fate of advanced preparation are both significant and complex. By cultivating development, helping feasible change, and ensuring that reasonableness and inclusivity illuminate data direction, pioneers and policymakers can assist with fathoming the full reasonability of advanced applied sciences in schooling. As we are apparently going from now on, obviously visionary administration and steady insurance contracts will be key drivers in the development of computerized schooling, ensuring that it serves the cravings of novices in an always-impacting world.

A Source of Inspiration for Teachers, Technologists, and Policymakers

As we stand on the limit of another innovation in schooling, framed permanently through the powers of advanced development, it will become incumbent upon us—teachers, technologists, and policymakers—to notice the source of inspiration. This second, prosperous, conceivable, and full of difficulties needs an aggregate commitment to tackle the power of computerized tutoring to improve all students. This finishing-up section fills in as a clarion call, encouraging partners all through the educational range to connect profoundly with the conceivable outcomes and obligations presented with the guidance of the computerized getting-to-know-unrest.

Embracing the Chances of Advanced Schooling: The computerized age manages the cost of phenomenal conceivable outcomes to embellish educational access, commitment, and results. Instructors are alluded to as typifying these open doors, coordinating computerized hardware and resources into their training practices to cultivate a more powerful and comprehensive learning climate. Technologists, on their part, are entrusted with developing moderate choices that tackle the different needs of students, focusing on availability, ease of use, and scholastic worth. Policymakers ought to set expectations for computerized tutoring to prosper through strong regulation, financing, and insurance contracts that focus on decency and greatness.

Taking part in deep-rooted learning: The quick beat of mechanical substitute highlights the meaning of long-lasting learning for teachers, technologists, and policymakers alike. Instructors should constantly supplant their capabilities and educational methods to really use new applied sciences. Technologists need to remain sensitive to the developing needs of the scholarly local area; they need to be responsive and pertinent to ensure their enhancements. Policymakers need to stay informed about advanced propensities in educational innovation, ensuring that inclusion structures are versatile and forward-looking.

Adding to the Continuous Exchange on Computerized Schooling: The eventual fate of advanced preparation will be framed by the considerations and experiences of a huge neighborhood of partners. Participating in continuous correspondence about the objectives, difficulties, and conceivable outcomes of advanced tutoring is significant for ensuring that this future lines up with cravings and yearnings, everything being equal. This discourse should be comprehensive, drawing on the perspectives of instructors, understudies, guardians, technologists, and policymakers to make an all-encompassing, creative, and perceptive vision for the eventual fate of schooling.

Aggregate Liability to Guarantee Advantages for Each Understudy: The advanced dominating unrest holds the commitment of making tutoring more available, customized, and incredible than any time in recent memory. Understanding this commitment requires an aggregate devotion to ensuring that the benefits of computerized preparation are accessible to every understudy, no matter what their experience, capacity, or financial status. This involves never again exclusively bestowing the right of passage to science, but furthermore ensuring that advanced preparation is significant, connecting with, and meeting students' different requirements.

Taking everything into account, the source of inspiration for instructors, technologists, and policymakers is clear. Together, we really want to outfit the groundbreaking capability of computerized instruction, exploring the difficulties and holding onto the potential outcomes with foreknowledge, imagination, and a profound commitment to value. By working cooperatively, we can frame an eventual fate of tutoring that is rich with potential outcomes, ensuring that every single student has the gear and conceivable outcomes to find lasting success in a rising number of computerized universes. The ride ahead of time is our own to shape, directed by means of the common inventiveness and perceptiveness of a scholastic scene that uses the outstanding force of science to engage and illuminate.